Liberated Publishing

Presents:

How to manage life with a new perspective

8 Week Guide to a Healthier Lifestyle

Andrus D. Love, MS

LiberatedPublishing.com

Liberated Publishing Inc.
1860 Wilma Rudolph Blvd
Clarksville, TN 37040

Copyright © 2015 Andrus Love

Published by: Liberated Publishing Inc

All rights reserved. No part of this book may be reproduced in any form or by any means without the prior written consent of the Publisher, excepting brief quotes used in reviews.

The characters and events in this book are fictitious. Any similarities to real persons living or dead are coincidental and not intended by the author.

If you purchased this book without a cover, you should be aware that this book is stolen property. It was reported as "unsold and destroyed" to the Publisher and neither the Author nor the Publisher has received any payment for this "stripped book".

ISBN: 978-0-9895732-8-3

First Printing: April 2015

Things to help foster your positive feelings

*Exercise, Smile, Outings, Talk, Friendships,
Hobbies, Laughing, Family, Animals, Reminisce*

Table of Contents

The Real You………………………………...…………………	1
Recognizing Your Power……………………………………	3
Feeding Your Own Feelings………………………..…………..	5
Self Support……………………………………..…………………..	7
Steps to Problem Solving……………………………………..	9
Understanding Control…………………………………….…	11
Personal Tips to Minimizing Problems………………….	13
Recall & Application………………………………………....	15

Positive Self-Talk Week 1

The Real You

I see myself as….

The best thing about me….

I love to….

I am afraid to….

I need….

I feel uncomfortable when….

I wish I had the courage to….

Three words to describe myself are….

When I look in the mirror I see….

I like it when people….

Positive Self-Talk Week 2

Recognizing Your Power

The best thing I like about myself….

I can….

Something I do well is….

Three things that make me a good friend are….

I have accomplished….

I am working on improving….

I will….

I feel good when….

The most powerful person I know….

People respect me for….

Positive Self-Talk Week 3

Feeding Your Own Feelings

Trust
- Do what makes you feel happy
- Act on what you feel is right
- Pay attention to your thoughts and feelings

Praise
- Be proud of who you are
- Take pride in your achievements
- Do not try to be someone else
- Learn to enjoy your own company

Encouragement
- Identify and accept your strengths and
- Compliment yourself on a daily basis
- Learn new skills and develop your abilities

Positive Self-Talk Week 4

Self-Support

Recognize peer pressure
Respect other people and treat them right
Spend time with people who care about you
Do not criticize yourself for making mistakes
Express your feelings freely and respectfully
Appreciate compliments
Be your own best friend
Set realistic goals
Do not be afraid to say I Love You
Do things you enjoy

Problem Solving Week 5

Steps to Problem Solving

1. **_Describe the situation_**- what's going on.

2. **_Analyze the situation_**- why is it a problem, who does it affect and how many people are affected?

3. **_Identify what you want to accomplish_**- set a specific goal.

4. **_Compute a solution_**- list any options and determine the best route.

5. **_Develop a plan_**- how do I need to approach the situation, what resources are needed and develop a timeline.

6. **_Apply the plan_**- put your steps into action.

7. **_Evaluation_**- is the current plan working or is another plan needed?

8. **_Celebrate the success_**- decide what reward is reasonable.

Problem Solving Week 6

Understanding Control

Fighting	Other people problems
Jealousy	Lack of Fun
Weather	Personal Choices
My Anger	The Sun Shining
Prayer	Homelessness
Violence	Eating Healthy
Death	Permission to Laugh
Fire	Ask for Help
Forgiving	My Lying

1. Circle the thing you have control over
2. Put a "X" by the things you have no control over
3. Explain how you exhibit control over circled items
4. Reflect and or discuss

Positive Self-Talk Week 7

Personal Tips to Minimizing Problems

1. Seek assistance when needed

2. Be a Team Player

3. Realize people feel or view things differently

4. Give or accept suggestions in a Respectful manner

5. Think about your body language

6. Be considerate of others

7. Focus on the good points people make

8. Be able to listen

9. Be supportive, cooperative and friendly

10. Develop a "Pros and Cons" list: (what is for progress/what is against progress)

Problem Solving Week 8

Recall and Application

Recall: To remember (something) from the past.

Application: An act of putting to use.

Use weeks 5-7 in order to recall the techniques giving in order to apply them to your daily life! - Andrus

This book is aimed at producing positive vibes in the midst of a struggle. You are equipped with the tools to turn your life around. Do not be so quick to settle or accept; even Doctors get 2nd/3rd opinions!
- Andrus

Bless the World; Heal the Nation, Inc.

"We all have a hand to Play"

Andrus D. Love, MS
CONSULTANT

Clinical Psychology & Couseling
motivational speaker, trainer, poet

(334) 354-9745

andruslove@yahoo.com

Andrus D. Love is an educated mentor, visionary, trainer, author, poet as well as a compassionate leader. He has a lovely wife and four beautiful children. Andrus believes all people are important with unique qualities and distinctive characteristics. He strives to be an optimist in the midst of problematic times mixed with sorrowful situations; while enhancing individuals' knowledge of how to manage everyday life. The University of Alabama at Birmingham (U.A.B.) allowed him to gain a Bachelor's Degree in Criminal Justice/Sociology; which he completed in 2001. He also graduated from Troy University with honors in Clinical Psychology & Counseling to obtain a Master's Degree in 2011. Overall, Andrus uses his personal experiences to give others a different perspective in life that permits them to adapt and or overcome!

**Liberated Publishing Inc.
1860 Wilma Rudolph Blvd
Clarksville, TN 37040
info@liberatedpublishing.com
931-378-0500**

www.LiberatedPublishing.com

www.ingramcontent.com/pod-product-compliance
Lightning Source LLC
Chambersburg PA
CBHW071458070426
42452CB00040B/1883